AF271567

A Day With Mac

Emily Smith

Copyright © 2022

All Rights Reserved

Dedication

This book is dedicated to Katie Reynolds who paid for Mac's food and vet visits the first year of his life. I am sorry for you that things didn't work out for you to get Mac, but I'm very happy that things worked out for him to live with me forever! We love you, Tia!

Acknowledgment

A special thank you to Dr. Darryl Moore and the staff at Moore Veterinary Clinic for helping Mac stay healthy and for taking care of him when he got hurt.

About the Author

Emily lives on a farm in southwest Tennessee and has a sewing business - Sweet Creations by Emily. Sweet Creations by Emily. When she isn't working on the farm or sewing for customers she can usually be found sewing clothes for Mac, dressing and photographing him, holding him, or keeping his fans up to date on his adventures on his Facebook page - A Cute Cat Named Mac. A Cute Cat Named Mac

Hello, everyone! My name is Mac, and I am a very busy cat. Come on inside and I'll tell you about all of the things that I do.

When the sun shines in my window…

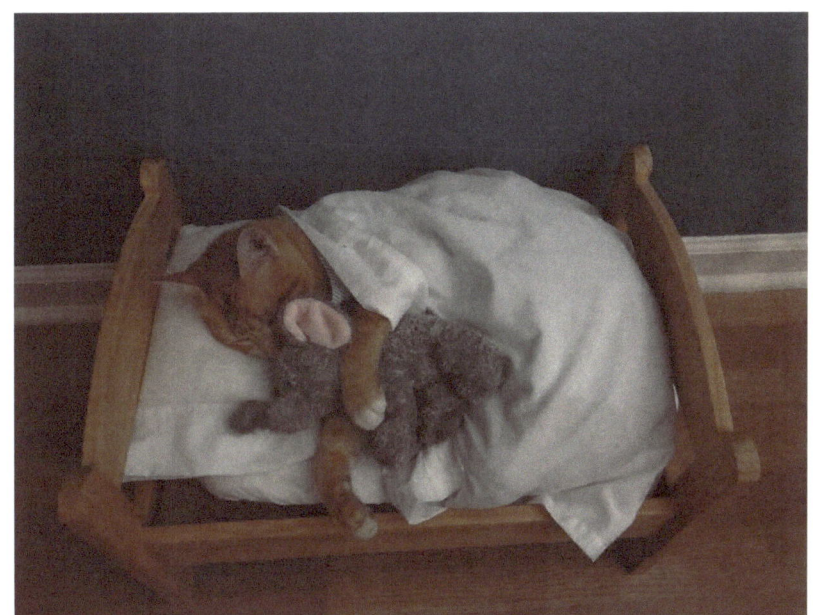

I know that it is time to get up!

I make my bed…

I get dressed…

I comb my hair…

That looks good! Now I am ready for the day!

Then it's time for breakfast. I love to eat!

After I eat breakfast

I wash my dishes

and brush my teeth.

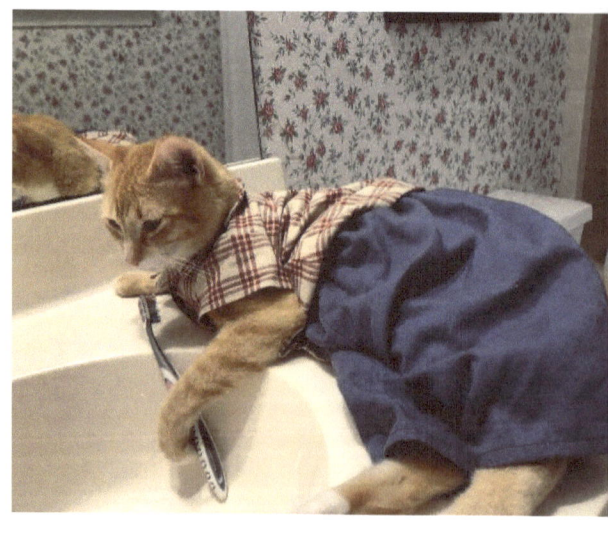

Then it is chore time.

I am big enough to do a lot of chores.

I know how to dust,

sweep,

mop,

clean the glass on the storm door,

wash the bathroom counter,

and scrub the bathtub.

When my chores are finished it's time for school.

Reading is my favorite part of school!

I like to use flash cards to study my math facts.

After school I love going to the library.

They have so many fun books there!

My favorite books have stories about cats.

I'm going to borrow "The Cat in the Hat" today.

I also have outside chores to do.

I know how to sweep the porch steps,

pull weeds,

water my flowers,

and mow the grass.

I have time to play every day, too.

When I'm in the house I play with my shapes toy,

my ring stacker,

my car carrier,

and my little camping set.

I also enjoy riding on my
stick horse.

Several days each week I practice the songs
I am learning to play on the piano.

I know that the more I practice
them the better they will
sound!

When I go outside to play I really like to swing.

I'm not brave enough, yet,

to slide down the big slide.

It's a lot of fun to drive around on my little car.

I can also help with the laundry.

First I use the clothes brush to get my fur off,

and then I load the washer.

I always check to make sure that I don't fill it too full.

When my clothes are clean and dry and I fold them neatly.

After dinner I read the book that I borrowed from the library.

As you can see, my favorite reading spot is on my bench in the yard.

When I am sick, or need a check-up,
I go to see Dr. Moore. He is a very good doctor!

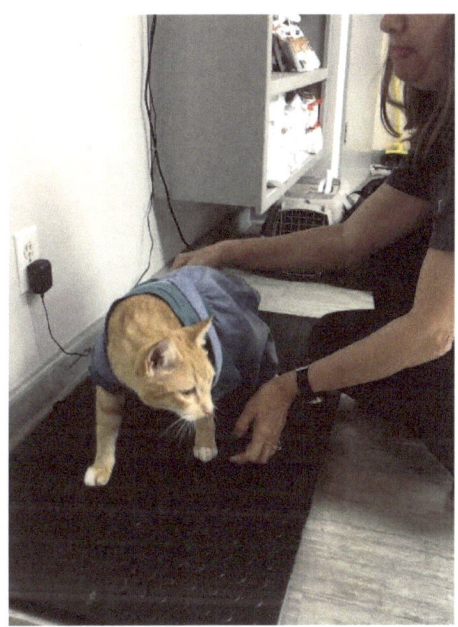

Mrs. Glenda puts me on the scale.
I weigh 10 pounds and 2 ounces.
I am a big boy!

Dr. Moore checks me all over to make sure that I am healthy.

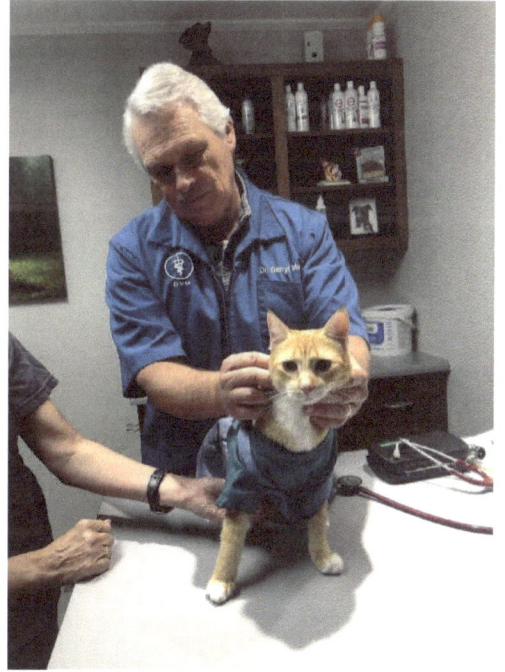

I am very brave when I get a shot. I sit still and it hurts for only one second.

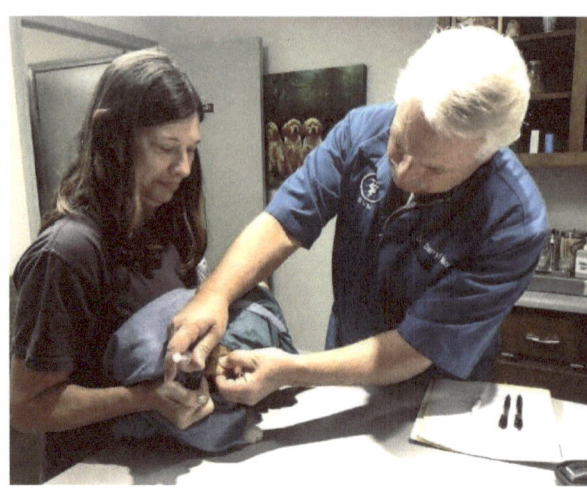

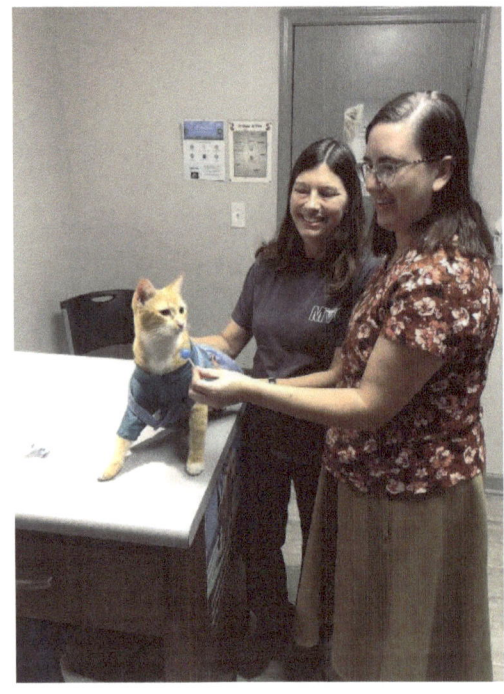

I got a sucker for being such a good boy at my check-up, but I didn't want to lick it when people were watching me.

When I got home I was happy to lick it.

I like suckers!

When the sun starts to go down I know it's time to get ready for bed.

I take a bath…

I put my pajamas on…

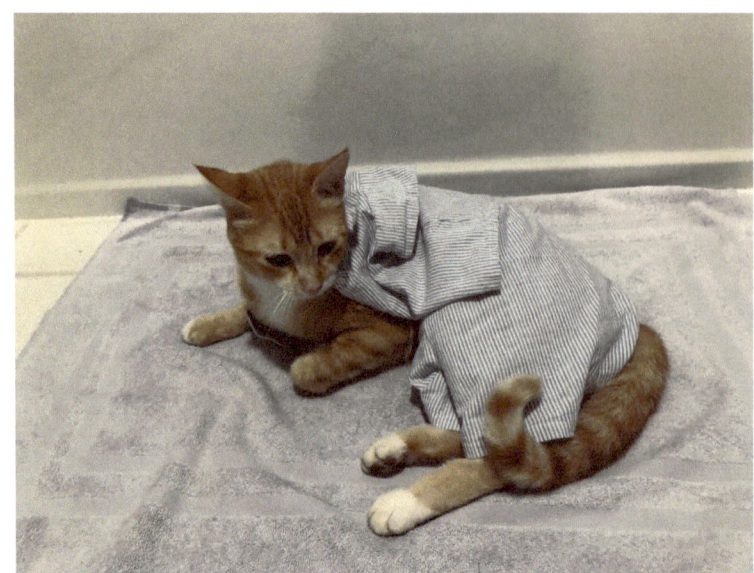

I brush my teeth…

And read a bedtime story.

Good night!

See you in the morning!

We hope you've enjoyed a day with Mac! This is just the beginning of Mac's adventures! Mac will be seeing you soon with more adventures and more fun books! Till then, goodbye! And see you soon!

Did you enjoy reading about all of the things that I do? Good! Look for more books that my mommy is planning to write about me soon! (She has to make me more outfits and take more pictures of me first!)

She wants to write a book about me when I was a baby.

She also wants to write a book about me trying to decide what I want to be when I grow up.

I could be a doctor and help my friends when they are sick…

or I could be a seamstress and sew clothes for my friends.

There are so many jobs that I could do!!

She would like to write a book about how different my life would be if I were a different animal, too.

My life sure would be different if I were a buffalo or a sheep!

Or a pig! Oink, oink!

I was a perfect angel for my dirty pig photo,

and my mommy let me have a few licks of a sucker as a treat when we were finished.

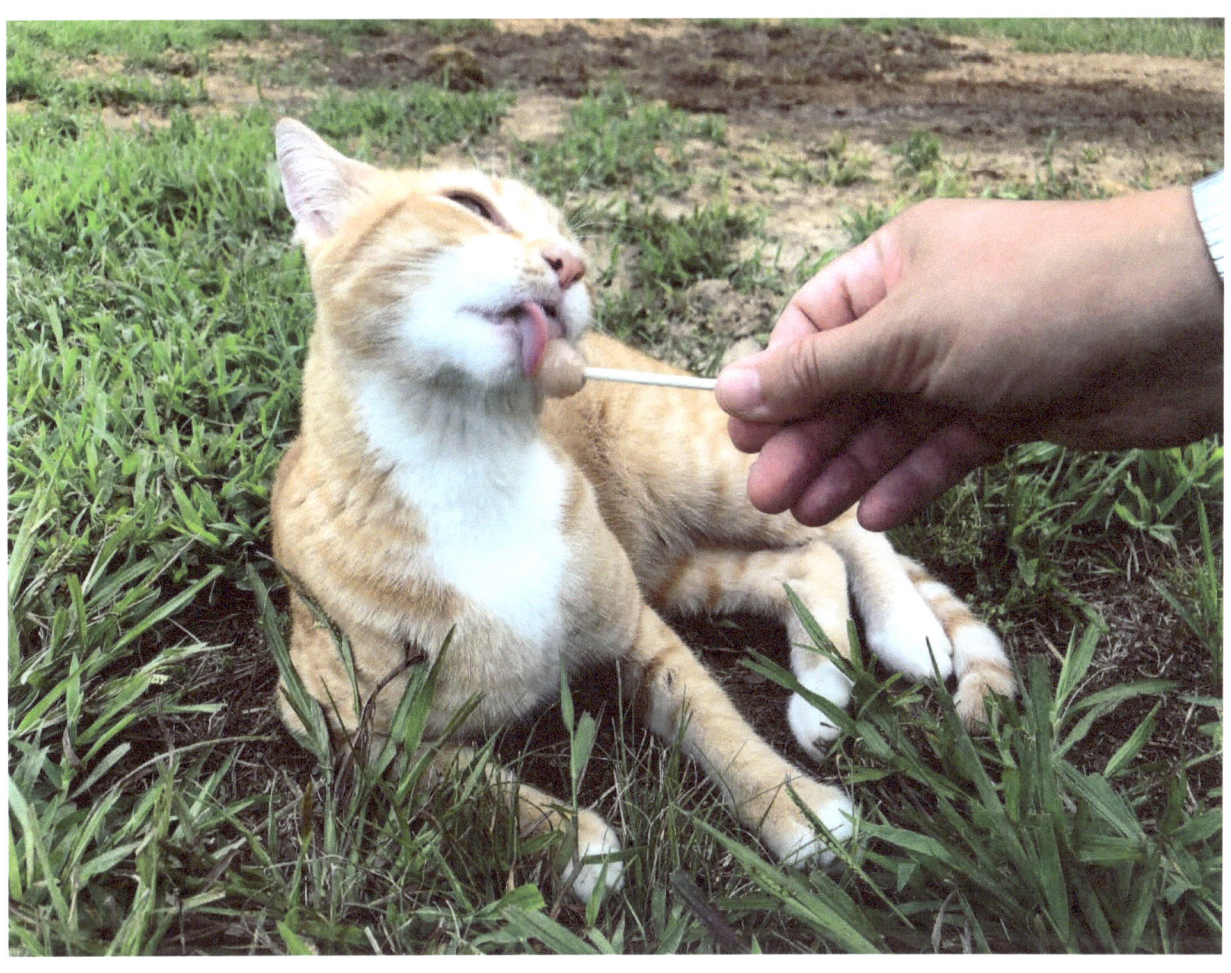

Milton Keynes UK
Ingram Content Group UK Ltd.
UKHW050633250424
441728UK00002B/23